Thai Insider:

An Insider's Guide to the Best of...

By Granville Kirkup and Robert Wisehart

Copyright

Thai Insider: Koh Samui

Copyright © 2017 by Granville Kirkup and Robert Wisehart. All rights reserved. This includes the right to reproduce any portion of this book in any form.

First edition, 2017

Rimping Publishing Company

Cover design by The Illustrated Author
www.theillustratedauthor.net

Disclaimer: Every effort was made to describe the information in this book accurately as of the publication date, but this information is subject to change by the companies and organizations concerned

Contents

1	Welcome to Koh Samui	5
2	Your First Visit to Thailand?	9
3	Thai Culture and Customs	13
4	Hotels	17
5	Getting About	25
6	Things to do	33
7	Restaurants	43
8	Bars and Clubs	51
9	Shopping	61
10	Sports & Fitness	67
11	Massage & Personal Care	75
12	Thai Food	81
13	Two or Three Days in Koh Samui	85
14	Staying Longer	93
15	Useful Information	97
16	Some Thai Phrases	103
17	Authors Bios	109
18	Acknowledgments	111
19	Further Reading	113

Thai Insider: Koh Samui

Welcome to Koh Samui

Koh Samui is Thailand's second largest island, after Phuket, and is just one hour by plane from Bangkok.

About 85 percent of the population is Buddhist. To avoid offense, tourists should dress respectfully, especially when visiting temples – remove your shoes and cover your shoulders when visiting a temple. So no halter tops or short shorts.

In this book you will learn about the best hotels and restaurants, from budget-friendly to five-star. We will tell you the best places to go and how to get there – both in town and for day trips to the rest of the island. We'll tell you the best places to shop, in malls or markets, and how not to get ripped off! We will tell you about the best bars and restaurants and where to listen to live music at night. As a bonus, there are hundreds of 'Insider tips' written by locals and frequent Koh Samui visitors.

Insider tip: There are current hotel and dining guides available for free at the airport when you first arrive.

Thai Insider: Koh Samui

All the Koh Samui history you really need to know

Koh Samui appeared on Chinese maps as far back as the 16th century. It was first settled by Thai fishermen about 1500 years ago. Fishing has remained an important island activity ever since, although now tourism is more important.

Until about 1940 Koh Samui had no roads or cars, and the island had little contact with the outside world. Tourism was unknown, as there was no convenient way to get to Koh Samui.

In the Second World War the Japanese briefly occupied the island, but were driven out by local fishermen in an angry battle. At least, that is how local fishermen tell the story today!

In the 1970s the island became popular with backpackers and budget travelers, and hotels & guest houses began to spring up. Now there are many three, four and five star hotels all over the island.

Geography

Koh Samui is the largest of a group of 80 islands in the Gulf of Thailand, about 22 miles from Surit Thani on the Thai mainland (one of the major cities in Southern Thailand), which is about 400 miles south of Bangkok. Other smaller islands in the group are Koh Phangan, Koh

Tao and Koh Taen. Koh Samui has about 35,000 inhabitants and an area of about 250 square kilometers, comparable to the Malaysian island of Penang.

About half of Koh Samui is mountainous, with the highest peak of Khao Yai in the center of the island. Vegetation ranges from the plentiful coconut palms to the ill-smelling Durian fruit trees.

The best time to visit

February through June is warm and the best time to visit, while July through October are the rainy months. November through January is cooler, but still a great time to visit. Temperatures range from 76F to 95F (25C to 35C). Koh Samui is usually warmer than Bangkok.

Insider tip: Songkran in mid-April is a festival that involves water fights and pelting locals and tourists with water and flour. If you are out and about you will get wet!

Today's Koh Samui includes a new shopping mall, trendy boutiques and shops, hotels, apartments and beachfront restaurants offering both Thai and western cuisine.

Enjoy your trip to Koh Samui – a unique Thai island to which you will want to return!

Thai Insider: Koh Samui

Your First Visit to Thailand?

Passport and visas

To enter Thailand you need a passport with the expiration date of at least six months after the end of your Thailand trip. A visa is not necessary if your stay is no longer than 30 days (29 nights). For longer stays you need to get a visa from a Thai embassy or consulate. Details can be found online at *Thaiembassy.com*.

A new METV visa was introduced in 2016. (Multiple Entry Tourist Visa). Visitors of any nationality can apply for a multiple-entry tourist visa valid for six months, with a stay per entry of up to 60 days. The cost of this visa is 5,000 baht. ($145 or £116)

Thailand is usually entered via Bangkok, but there are also direct flights to Koh Samui, Chiang Mai and Phuket. Some of these flights depart from Hong Kong (Bangkok Air) and Singapore (Silk Air). The flight to and from Bangkok takes about one hour.

Events and festivals

January: Samui Ride & Fun Festival. Biking and running.

April: Songkran New Year water celebrations and water fights. If you are out, you will get drenched by supersoakers!

May: Koh Samui Regatta. Sailing yachts.

June: Queen's Cup Golf Tournament.

July: King Vajiralongkorn's birthday, July 28, 1952.

November: Loi Krathong. Can be translated as 'To float a basket', which comes from the tradition of floating decorated floating baskets traditionally made from banana leaves called 'Krathong' in rivers and ponds. In Samui the festival is also celebrated by launching thousands of 'khom loi' fire balloons into the sky. The party lasts for three days.

Insider tip: Khom loi (fire balloons) used to be sent into the sky by the thousands on all three days, but a 2016 law restricted this to 9pm – midnight on the main day of Loi Krathong only, as Khom Loi can be a danger to aircraft.

December: Former King Bhumipol's birthday, December 5, 1927. The former King is still much revered.

Religion

Buddhism (95%). Other religions include Muslim (3.8%) Hinduism (0.1%) and Christianity (0.5%).

Language

The language spoken is Thai, with some regional differences. English is widely spoken in hotels and restaurants.

Food and drink

Thai food can be very spicy, but Koh Samui's food is usually less spicy than that of the northeast or the south. Many restaurants also serve western food.

Don't drink Thai tap water, even to clean your teeth. Use bottled water. Water and iced served in restaurants are usually OK – certainly in the main tourist spots.

Shopping

Shopping options range from market stalls to air-conditioned malls, like Central Festival. There are many bargains to be had, and haggling is expected in markets and smaller stores. (Not in shopping malls.)

Insider tip: When haggling, be relaxed and cheerful. Smile or laugh at the first price offered, and offer about half. Expect to end up around two thirds of the first offered price. Don't haggle down to the last 10 baht – that is only 30 cents. The vendors need to make a living!

Collectors can find antiques from Thailand, Burma, Cambodia and Laos. Be warned, there are many fakes. It's forbidden to take any Buddha image out of Thailand without a permit.

Insider tip: If you mail a box home they will open the box and search it at the post office. They will remove any Buddha images, liquids (even hair spray) and sharp objects like scissors.

Thai Baht

The exchange rate for Thai baht fluctuates, but for this book a rate of approximately 35 baht to the US dollar is used, or 43 baht to the British pound.

You can exchange your local currency for Thai baht at many 'change money' places in town (for example, there are several near Green Mango Street). There are also many ATMs, which will dispense Thai baht.

Thai Culture and Customs

Thailand is a fun and easy-going country, but a basic understanding of the country's culture and customs makes travel more interesting and helps to avoid giving offense.

Head, feet and shoes

The head is the most sacred part of the body in Thailand, so do not touch people on the head, even children.

The feet are the 'unclean' part of the body, so avoid pointing your feet at people, especially monks if you are sitting in a temple. Tuck them underneath you or fold your legs to one side.

Remove your shoes before going into a house or temple building. Hotel staff will always remove their shoes before coming into your room. Do the same if you are 'just looking' at a hotel room. For this reason, slip-on shoes for men are best in Thailand.

The King

The king is much revered in Thailand (they usually refer to him as 'my King'), so always be respectful to the king and the royal family. Almost every home and business has a photograph of the king on the wall. The late king was particularly admired. There are strict *Lese Majeste* laws making it a serious offence to speak negatively about the king or the royal family. So to be safe, it's best not to discuss the king or the royal family at all when in Thailand.

Buddha and monks

Most Thais are Buddhist, and most Thai men are monks at some time in their life. They wear the traditional saffron robes and do not eat after midday. To give to a monk is said to 'make merit'. They will not thank you, as your merit is thanks enough. Women may not touch monks.

Buddha images (statues) are sacred. Do not touch them on their head, or with your feet. In temples, do not wear shorts, and women should keep their shoulders covered.

Most businesses (and hotels) have either a 'spirit house' outside, or a niche on an inside wall. They give flowers, food and water to the spirits every day. Thais are very superstitious and they believe that sprits of the deceased live in their houses. The daily offerings are to make peace with the spirits.

The Wai

The traditional Thai greeting is the wai – hands together as if in prayer, and bow slightly. It does not mean 'hello', but is a mark of respect, so in general do not wai back, especially to doormen etc. However, Thais are used to farangs (that's us) waiing back, so it's not a big error. Best to smile back politely. It's OK to wai to monks, and the king, should you meet him.

Insider tip: You may hear Thais call us 'falangs' also. They often pronounce the letter 'r' as an 'l'.

No losing face

For Thais it is important to keep their temper and not lose face. So if your hotel reservation is lost, the best thing to do is to smile politely and insist that they find it. Do not get angry as that is much frowned upon, and will not get you anywhere.

Age is respected, 'No' is not

Thais respect people their elders – that is why Thais may ask 'how old are you?" (No need to provide an answer). They also may sometimes ask 'how much do you earn?'

That is not impolite in Thailand, and the correct answer is 'not enough!' Thais will generally avoid responding to a question with 'no', so if you ask a question like 'Do you have any children?', they may answer 'not yet'. You ask, "Do you like beer?" they answer 'A little." That means no.

Thai food and bottled water

Thai food in Thailand is a bit different from the American and British version of Thai food except in big hotels – it tends to be hotter. Be cautious about eating from roadside stalls. Drink only bottled water in Thailand, even to brush your teeth. Thais do not use chopsticks when eating, but a spoon and fork. Except that they use chopsticks for noodle soup. Go figure.

Thai Values

Buddhism shapes Thai values to a large extent, but the concept of fun, or *sanuk*, is very important to Thais also. You will also hear Thais say *'mai pen rai'*, which means 'that's OK', or 'it doesn't matter'. Thais are usually a relaxed and easygoing people.

Koh Samui Hotels

Hotel guide price ranges:
$ 2,000 – 5,000 baht   ($50 - $140,   £46 - £116)
$$ 5,000 – 10,000 baht   ($140 - $280, £116 - £232)
$$$ 10,000 – 15,000 baht   ($280 - $420, £232 - £348)
$$$$ 15,000 – 20,000 baht   ($420 - $560, £348 - £465)

There are many backpacker hostels and guest houses in Koh Samui, but we do not cover them in this book. Our hotel price ranges start at about $50 a night. Lonely Planet, for example, covers less expensive hostels.

Budget Hotels

Deva Samui Resort ($) Situated in the Big Buddha area, next to Samui Boat Lagoon, and close to Bophut Fisherman's Village. 79 spacious rooms in Thai contemporary style with refrigerator and flat screen TV. *By The Sea* restaurant serves both Thai and western menus. Spa, children's activities, fitness center. 69/34 Moo 5, Bophut. 077 417-300. *Devasamui.com*

Ark Bar Beach Resort ($). A one-stop party destination in the heart of Chaweng. A three star resort property situated right on the beach. Three swimming pools, beach club and two swim-up pool bars. Live music and fire shows. A DJ from 2pm. Several rooms types including Superior and Deluxe to Premier Deluxe Seaview. Air-conditioning, en-suite bathroom and mini-bar. Tour desk. 159/89 Moo 2, Chaweng Beach Road. 077 961-333. Ark-bar.com info@ark.bar.com.

Insider tip: The deluxe seaview rooms overlook the party pool, right in the middle of the action and music. Great if that is what you are looking for. Otherwise, book a different room type. This is a fun hotel, but probably not ideal for families.

Chaweng Garden Beach Resort. ($) A family-owned Chaweng resort opened in 1990. Right on the beach, with all of the walkways covered by sand – you can walk barefoot all day long! Standard rooms in a two-storey garden building, garden bungalows and beach front bungalows. Two restaurants – *Sue's Ocean Restaurant*, breakfast lunch and dinner on the beach, and *Samui Wine Oasis Restaurant*, for Thai and International food. Chaweng Beach Road. 077 960-394. Chawenggarden.com Sales@Chawenggarden.com.

Chaweng Cove Beach Resort. ($) Large beachfront resort in the quiet southern part of Chaweng. 101 cozy guest rooms: Deluxe whirlpool room, Deluxe balcony room, Deluxe garden bungalow or Beachfront pool villa. ($$). Free airport transfer. *The Cove* restaurant, all-day beachfront dining. Pool bar.   17/4 Moo 3, Chaweng Beach Road. 077 422-509. *Chawengcove.com.*

Insider tip: It's a 15 minute walk from the hotel to the main part of town, or you can take a taxi.

Boutique Hotels

Poppies ($$) At the south end of Chaweng Beach Road, a boutique hotel with 24 individual Thai style cottages, one guest room per cottage. A winding path leads through the grounds to the bar and excellent restaurant near the beach. (See the restaurant listing). Small spa. The rooms have both air conditioning and fan, while the bathrooms have a private screened garden open to the sky. There is a sister hotel in Bali. PO Box 1, Chaweng. 077 422-419. *Poppiessamui.com.*

Insider tips: The bathrooms are not air-conditioned, so ladies may want to keep cosmetics in the cool of the bedroom. There is wi-fi and an Internet room / business center with printer for guest use. This is a good choice for a mid-price boutique hotel.

Sala Samui ($$$). Beachfront boutique hotel half way between Chaweng & Big Buddha / Fisherman's Village. Modern design with white walls and big windows. Room types: Deluxe balcony, Garden pool villa, Sala pool villa and 1 and 2 bedroom pool villas. *Sala Samui* restaurant, with breakfast buffet and Thai and International lunch and dinner. *Beach bar*. *Pangaea*, a small Italian restaurant owned by the hotel on the road nearby. 10/9 Moo 5, Baan Plai Laem. 077 245-888. *Salaresorts.com/Samui.* At the time of writing there is also **Sala Samui Chaweng Beach Resort** under construction in Chaweng.

Insider tips: 20 minutes from town. There are very large window walls in this resort, in the bedrooms and bathrooms - there are drapes which some guests feel the need to keep closed!

Mid-Range Hotels

Amari Koh Samui ($$) A modern beachfront hotel just north of town on Chaweng Beach Road. Over 180 rooms in nine room types, spread over three wings of the resort. Four restaurants and bars, including the Italian restaurant *Prego*, over the road (see restaurant listings). Three swimming pools, spa and kids club. Travel desk and car rentals on-site. Just three km from Samui airport. 14/3 Chaweng Beach Road. 077 300-306 *Amari.com/Koh-Samui.*

Insider tip: Some of the rooms are on the other side of the road, where there is a second pool. Request the main building if that is your preference. This is a good choice for a mid-range hotel.

Melati Beach Resort & Spa ($$$) On Thongson Bay in the northern part of Samui. 77 contemporary rooms and suites, in a garden. Two swimming pools and spa, fitness center and library. *The View* restaurant, beachfront all-day dining. *Kan Sak Thong* restaurant, close to the resort's waterfall, authentic Thai and French cuisine. *Sea View* bar. Round-the-clock room service. There is a shuttle bus service to Chaweng several times a day. 077 913-400. *MelatiBeachResort.com.*

Insider tip: This hotel is a 15 minute drive from town.

Le Meridien Koh Samui Resort & Spa. ($$$) Situated in Lamai on Koh Samui's east coast. 77 suites and private pool villas in a Thai contemporary style. Spa, airport transfers, shuttle to Chaweng, baby sitting, fitness center, daily activities. Restaurants and bars: *Latest Recipe*, all day dining, open to the ocean. *Ocean Pier*, a unique floating restaurant on a pier. *Latitude 09*, drinks and tapas until late. *Plunge bar*, pool bar. 146/24 Moo 4, Lamai Beach. 077 960-888. *Lemeridienkohsamui.com*

OZO Chaweng Samui. ($$$) Trendy beachfront resort close to the center of Chaweng. 208 rooms available in six types with modern minimalist décor. Restaurants:

Eat, all day dining, and *Stacked*, a well-known restaurant serving burgers, steaks and seafood. Happy hours 5-7pm and 10-11pm. Chaweng Beach Road. 077 334-300. *Ozohotels.com/Chaweng-Samui*

Up-Market Hotels

Koh Samui has several up-market hotels, mostly outside of town. Here are three of the best:

Four Seasons Resort ($$$$) 45 minutes outside of town in the north west of the island, beyond Big Buddha and Bophut. Built on steep terrain, rooms and villas along winding paths, which lead down to the beach. Large marble bathrooms with walk-in showers. Three restaurants: *Koh Thai Kitchen* - on a hilltop with great views of the ocean, *Pla Pla* – Mediterranean, and *CocCoRum* – lunch and dinner and rum cocktails. There are also two bars, *Koh Bar* and *CoCoRum* bar, which also offers cocktail classes for 1800 baht, under the watchful eye of the head bartender! Private beach and pleasure cruisers. 219 Moo 5, Angthong. 077 243-000. *Fourseasons.com*

Insider tips: A long way from Chaweng. The footpaths between the rooms are very steep, so request a buggy (golf cart) to take you to your room, to the beach, or to one of the restaurants. There is a free shuttle service to town several times a day. Four Seasons hotels are always excellent.

Anantara Lawana ($$$) There are two Anantara hotels north of Chaweng, and this is the closest, about half a mile from the main town. Situated on the beach, with villas on winding paths. Two restaurants, *Ocean Kiss*, an all-day open air restaurant with Asian and Western menus, and *Tree Tops*, private dining among the tree tops of the resort. *Pool bar* with snacks. Spa, private boat charters, Thai boxing classes, cocktail mixing classes. 92/1 Moo 2, Bophut. 077-960-333. *Anantara.com*

***Insider tip*:** If you go to Ocean Kiss, the beach side restaurant, call for a buggy (gold cart). That will take you part of the way, and you walk the rest of the way to the restaurant down a winding path. At night this can be very dark, and there are steps, so bring a flashlight or your phone!

Anantara Bophut ($$$) Close to Fisherman's Village, with windsurfing, spa and yoga. 106 resort rooms, tennis court, children's club. Restaurants include *Full Moon* (contemporary Samuian char grill cuisine), *High Tide* (Thai and International) and *Library* (afternoon tea). *Eclipse bar* (cocktail lounge in a lush garden). Private boat charters. Snorkelling and diving. 30 minutes from town. 99/9 Bophut Bay. 077-428-300. *Anantara.com*

Insider tip: Bophut's Fisherman's Village has many shops, bars and restaurants, suitable for families, within easy reach of this resort. The Anantara group of hotels give excellent service.

Getting About

Walking

Koh Samui is a good island for walking – if you can avoid the potholes and motorbikes on the sidewalks in the center of town! The central area of Chaweng is quite large, but can easily be walked. However sidewalks, which are not always present in some parts of the island, can be blocked by parked motorbikes so be prepared to walk in the street.

Walking tips

- It can get hot! Wear a hat.
- Bring a bottle of water.
- Wear comfortable walking shoes. Dress appropriately for temple visits, covering the arms and legs.
- Don't plan to do too much in one day.

Insider tip: There are pedestrian crossings, but, if they have no red light to stop traffic, use them at your own risk! Traffic rarely stops. Best to wait for a break in the traffic and cross quickly.

Songthaews but no Tuk Tuks

If you are used to Bangkok, Pattaya or Chiang Mai you will notice that there is something missing in Koh Samui. There are no tuk tuks! (The small motorized three wheeled vehicles.) However, there are plenty of songthaews.

Songthaews (song taws) are the colored pickups with two benches in the back seen all over town. The usual rate is 20 baht, so flag down a Songthaew and tell the driver where you are going. You can flag them anywhere, and they often congregate outside popular restaurants.

If the driver says 'yes', get into the back of the pickup. He may go to other places on the way, and pick up other riders. When he reaches your destination, ring the bell, get out, and pay him 20 baht.

If he says 'no', he is not going your way, so step aside and find another Songthaew. He may want to negotiate the rate, particularly if the vehicle is empty. That is typically 60 to 100 baht ($2 - $3). If you negotiate a rate, you have a 'private hire' and the driver will take you directly to your destination.

Getting About

Inside tip: There is no scheduled bus service in Koh Samui.

Yellow Taxis

Yellow and maroon cabs are easy to spot all over the island, particularly in Chaweng and the popular beach towns. They used to be called 'Taxi Meters' but few or no taxis use their meters nowadays. Rates are 200 baht to take you from Chaweng to your hotel in town, and go up from there. Rates are higher in the evening and at night. Be sure to negotiate the fare before setting off.

Taxi Service web site: Book a taxi from the airport to your hotel, or around the island: *Samuitaxi.com*

Insider tip: Motorbike taxis can also be found in Samui by looking for riders in brightly colored vests. They can zip through traffic and avoid hold ups. You sit on the back of the motorbike. As with regular taxis, you need to agree the fare before you set off.

Bicycle rental

Bicycles as a form of transportation have been around in Koh Samui for decades, particularly as bicycle rickshaws. (There are still a few about). You can rent a good mountain bike for about 80 baht a day. However, the island is hilly and that can make for an exhausting ride!

Some hotels and guest houses provide bikes to guests for free. There are also several bike rental shops offering reasonable rates. You may be asked for a deposit or to leave your passport. A passport copy or a passport card, is usually accepted. Make sure to get a bike lock.

Motorbike and scooter rental

There are many places to rent a scooter or motorbike in Koh Samui Mai. There are motorbike hire shops, and some resorts, backpacker hostels and monthly accommodation places either have their own scooters or can quickly obtain one with a phone call.

It's best to rent from a place that speaks English. Some places take credit cards, but not all. So bring cash.

Renting a scooter

There are three main types of scooter:

- Fully automatic – no gears
- Semi automatic – gears but no clutch
- Manual – gears and clutch

Getting About

The fully automatic is the easiest to ride. Most scooters come in the 110cc, 115cc and 125cc size. The Honda Dream / Wave is a good choice, a 110 – 125cc four-stroke single cylinder scooter.

Before taking the scooter to a complete visual check and photograph any scrapes or damage on your phone. Select the newest bike that they have. Take the bike for a ride and check the brakes and acceleration. Make sure that you have the number of the bike rental shop in case of an accident or a flat tire.

You will be asked to leave a security deposit or your passport as security. It is best to pay the deposit, as you should always carry your passport with you. You can leave a passport copy with them. Do opt for insurance, but make sure that it is full coverage – some insurance coverage requires you to pay for any damage. Remember to drive on the left!

Motorbike rental

Kawasaki and Honda now manufacture bigger bikes in Thailand, in the 250, 500 and 650cc range. Be aware of your limitations – it is not necessary to ride a big bike to enjoy the scenery.

Insider tip: Thailand can be a dangerous country to drive in if you are not cautious. So don't learn to drive a scooter or motorbike here! Make sure that your travel insurance included motorbike driving – some do not.

Helmet laws

It is mandatory for you and any passenger to wear a helmet if you are riding a motorbike or scooter. This is quite strictly enforced and there are police checkpoints where they will give you a ticket if you are not wearing a helmet.

Car rental

Cars can be rented from many places in Koh Samui, but if you are arriving and departing from the airport, the airport car rental offices are the most convenient, though they may cost more. The five car rental offices at the airport are Avis, Budget, Europcar, Hertz and Sixt.

Your hotel may also arrange for a rental car. A typical cost is 1,000 – 2,000 baht a day. ($30 - $60). Hotel car rentals usually have the car on-site and require little documentation. You can pay by cash or credit card.

If you intend to explore the island a lot, particularly the hilly interior, a 4 x 4 is recommended.

Getting About

Insider tip: If you are given a choice of car, choose one with a red license plate. Brand new cars have red license plates!

Driving in Thailand

Koh Samui roads are busy and there are bikes and scooters everywhere. The traffic takes a little getting used to, and of course they drive on the left. Local drivers behave as if red stop lights are 'just a suggestion'! Traffic lights can take several minutes to change in your favor, so when the light turns red it is not unusual to see 3, 4 or 5 cars and motorbikes go through on red. Cars and bikes often turn in front of you, even if you have the right of way. So drive defensively and be aware that Thai drivers seem to make their own rules.

For example: You are turning right from the right turn lane, which is on the left side of the road. It is not unusual to see motorbikes pull up alongside, on the right, in the middle of the road. Hopefully they will be turning right with you, but no, they may well be going straight ahead. So watch out!

Parking

Thai drivers invariably back into parking lot spaces because it's easier to pull out in the limited space available. Also, cars blocking other cars in a busy lot is normal in Thailand. The cars are left in neutral, and can be easily pushed out of the way, sometimes with the help of the guard, if there is one.

Red and white check curbs mean 'no parking' and the rule is tightly enforced. Park there and you may get clamped, with a ticket on the windscreen.

There is not normally paid parking on the street, but there are some off-street paid parking lots, often behind shops and restaurants. The parking fee is usually 50 baht. ($1.50)

Insider tip: If you see an accident (most likely a tumble from a motorbike or scooter), it's tempting to stop and see if all is OK. That is not a good idea. In the confusion following an accident, particularly if the police are called, any wealthy western person (farang) on the scene (that is you) is likely to be blamed for the accident. The assumption is that you have plenty of money to pay for the damage! All of this takes place in Thai which you probably don't understand. So unless you are involved, leave road accidents to Thai motorists and go on your way.

Things to do in Koh Samui

Elephant Safari tours

In Thailand, elephants were used in warfare and logging for hundreds of years. Nowadays their numbers are in decline, and elephant camps, where elephants are protected and well cared for, make these fine animals available for tourists. There is a close relationship between the elephant and his or her mahout (who takes daily care of the elephant) – often for life. There are several elephant camps in Koh Samui. This is one of the best known.

Namuang Safari Samui

Situated in the center of the island, but they will pick you up from your hotel, usually around 8am. An 'elephant safari' may include:

- Elephant trekking

- Visit to Namuang waterfall, 80 meters high

- Baby elephants bathing

- Baby elephants at play
- Visit to the monkeys at work, picking up coconuts
- Buffet lunch

Adult 1,400 baht. Children 1,100 baht.

25/11 M2 Namuang. 077 424-098.

Namuangsafari@gmail.com

Temples

Some tips for visiting temples

- Dress in appropriate clothing, covering your arms and legs.
- Before entering a temple, turn off your mobile phone, remove your hat and shoes.
- When greeting a monk, do so with a 'wai'. Place your palms together at chest level, as if in prayer. Bow slightly. The monk will not wai back.
- Be prepared to make a donation in one of the offering boxes. 20 or 100 baht is appropriate.
- Most temples are open during daylight hours.

Big Buddha Temple

Big Buddha Temple (Wat Phra Yai) is the best known landmark in Koh Samui. Located in Koh Samui's eastern corner – close to the Fisherman's Village of Bophut, it is situated on a small rocky island, reached by a causeway. The 12 meter high seated Buddha statue was built in 1972. There is a steep flight of steps leading up to the Buddha, but if that is a problem, there is a quite good view from the bottom of the steps.

Location: Just off route 4171, the northern road between Chaweng and Bophut / Fisherman's Village.

Insider tip: If you are on the 4171 road and you come to Fisherman's Village, you have gone too far! The turn off to Big Buddha is a sharp turn to the right, a couple of miles before Fisherman's Village.

Wat Plai Laem

Wat Plai Laem is a Buddhist temple inland close to Big Buddha and is known for its striking 18-arm image of Guanvin, the Goddess of Mercy and Compassion. There are some other large figures in the grounds.

Location: From Big Buddha, turn left onto the main road, and after about half a mile, take the first left turn. Continue past the school on the right, and turn right into the temple grounds.

Laem Sor Pagoda

At the end of Bang Kao beach in southern Koh Samui. The entrance is guarded by two big warrior statues with large swords. A great photo opportunity!

Location: Take road 4169 to road 4170 and turn left. Then left onto Laem Sho Road.

Wat Khunaram

This temple is unique because it contains the mummified body of a monk in a glass case! Monk Luang Pho Poo Rerm died at the age of 87 in 1976 while meditating, and ever since his body has been displayed in an upright glass case in the temple. It is remarkably well preserved. Not for the squeamish!

Luang Pho Poo Rerm was the temple principal and sub-district principal for 30 years until his passing. He led a solitary life of meditation and ate a single meal each day for most of his life.

Location: On route 4169 (the ring road) about six kilometers west of Lamai Beach.

Insider tip: The mummified monk is not in the main temple building but can be found in a smaller temple building to the left of the main entrance. A (live) monk is usually in attendance to give blessings and accept donations.

Insider tip: **'What's What in a Wat'**, by Carol Stratton is a good book about Buddhist temples in general. Published by Silkworm books in Chiang Mai. *Silkwormbooks.com*

Grandpa and Grandma Rocks

These rocks near Lamai Beach are the subject of much mirth and amusement. They are known as the Hin Ta (Grandpa) and Hin Yai (Grandma) rocks and look, respectively, like male and female genitalia.

The legend of Hin Ta and Hin Yai is that they lived in the southern province of Nakhon Si Thammarat with a son who had come of age to marry. They decided to sail to a neighboring province to ask for the hand of the daughter of a man named Ta Monglai. The boat capsized and both Grandpa and Grandma were lost at sea, turning into rocks to show the would-be bride their true intentions.

Location: Off route 4169 about two kilometers from Lamai Beach. The path to the rocks passes through a small village where snacks, drinks and postcards of the rocks are for sale.

Things to do in Koh Samui

Day Trip to Koh Phangan

Safari Boat. An all-day trip to the neighboring island of Koh Phangan. They pick you up from your hotel around 8am, and after a light breakfast take the 20 minute speedboat ride to Koh Phangan island. There you can ride and feed elephants, visit a waterfall, zipline and see a Thai dancing show, relax on the beach or try archery. Lunch is provided. Speedboat and minivan transfer back to your hotel. 1,900 baht per person, children 1,490 baht. 077 447-700. *Safariboat.info. info@safariboat.info*.

Golf, Tennis, Mountain Bikes, Ziplining

Look for descriptions of these and other activities in the 'Sports and Fitness' chapter.

City Tours

Island Safari City Tour. City tours around the island. Most tours are about six hours, and hit all of the highlights – Big Buddha, Grandpa and Grandma rocks, elephant show, etc. 600 – 800 baht. 077 425-563. *Islandsafaritour.com*.

Off-Road Tours

Samui Off Road Mountain Tour Company. Offers a variety of off-road tours, like Eco tour – temples and elephants, mountain tours, waterfalls by off-road vehicles and ATV tours. They will pick you up from your hotel, usually around 8am.   077 424-098. *Namuangsafarisamui.com*

Namuang Jungle Trip. Offers similar tours, and paintball! About 700-1,200 baht. Situated close to the mummified monk temple.   077 424-729 *Samuijungletrip.com*

Indoor Skydiving

EasyFly, situated at Chaweng Lake. Indoor skydiving daily from 1pm until 9pm. A modern and secured vertical wind tunnel that simulates true freefall conditions. For kids and adults. Starts at 1,500 baht. *Easykart.net*

Cooking Schools

Thai cooking is fun and not that difficult to execute. There are many cooking schools in Koh Samui. Class times are usually from 90 minutes to three hours. In most classes, the students will visit a local market with the instructor, to select and buy the ingredients.

Some of the larger hotels offer cooking classes, or you can choose from one of these three:

Pai Cooking Class. By appointment, on Chaweng Beach Road opposite Samui Resotel Resort. 086 952-3672

Samui Institute of Thai Culinary Arts (SITCA). Chaweng Beach. One of the most popular cooking schools in Samui. English-speaking instructors. Twice daily classes at 11am and 4pm. 077 413-172

Sonja's Thai Cooking Class. Maenam Beach. Classes are offered in English and German and include a soup, starter, main course and curry. 089 725-5610.

Koh Samui Restaurants

Ordering

Most Samui restaurants cater to westerners and have menus in both Thai and English. The servers usually understand limited English, so try to speak slowly and clearly. If they have difficulty understanding your order, it is helpful to point to the item on the menu, where it also is written in Thai. Thai customers will often say 'one' after ordering an item, or your server may ask 'one?' after you order.

Wine and Drinks

Alcoholic drinks and a choice of soft drinks are available in most restaurants, as well as coffee and tea. Because of taxes, wine can be much more expensive in Thailand than at home. When there are wines by the glass often only one red and one white is offered. Beer comes in two sizes, 'large' and 'small'. The water in restaurants is safe to drink.

How was your meal?

Your waiter or waitress may ask, "And what about your dinner?" Sometimes they ask this when you are just starting your meal. The correct response is *"Di maak"* (very good), or *"Aroi maak"* (very delicious).

Insider tip: Thais will always respond with *Di maak* or *Aroi maak,* no matter what they think of the meal. To say anything less would not be polite. But you can show your true feelings by how much enthusiasm (or lack of it) you put into using one of these two phrases.

Tipping

In Thailand it is not necessary to leave a 'percentage' tip in most restaurants. In very good restaurants or a nice hotel you may still want to leave 10-15%, but in most restaurants Thais tip 20 or 100 baht. Some more expensive restaurants (often in hotels) already have a service charge of 10% added. In that case it is usual to leave 100 baht as a little extra.

Paying your bill

To ask for the bill, ask for *Gep taang (*followed by *krub* if you are male, or *kaa* if you are female*)* in Thai, or 'check bill', in English (which Thais will pronounce as 'check bin'), which will be understood. They present the bill, you hand over your cash or credit card, and they take it to the cash desk. There is always a central cash desk where bills are processed and change made. The server brings your credit card or change back to the table. Be patient because this can take several minutes.

Some Restaurant Choices

Dr Frogs – South of Chaweng Beach, on the main road, on one of the most scenic viewpoints of Samui. Probably the best restaurant in town , with Italian and Thai menus, but it is known mostly for its superb Italian dishes. Can get full every night, so best to book. Extensive wine list. Mostly English speaking staff. Reservations suggested. Can be expensive. Lunch and dinner. Dinner hours are 7pm – 11pm. 077 448 505.

Insider tips: Request an ocean view table. There is limited car parking in front of the restaurant, and upon leaving it is necessary to back out onto the main road. Or take a taxi there and they will get you a taxi back to your hotel. Either way, this restaurant is well worth it.

Hard Rock Café – Chaweng Beach Road near Soi Green Mango. A recent addition to the Samui dining scene, the

Hard Rock Café features a shop selling Hard Rock merchandise, and the walls are adorned with rock memorabilia. Air conditioned restaurant and large outdoor patio with a stage and couches. Large American menu. Good bar. Great potato skins. Deserts large enough for two! Opens at 11.30am and the restaurant closes at 12.30am, although snacks are available until 2am. 077 901 208-9.

Insider tip: Although the restaurant is open most of the day, it doesn't really start moving until about 6pm. The nearby bars in Soi Green Mango do not open until 8 – 9pm.

Prego – Chaweng Beach Road, near the Amari Hotel, a few minutes north of town. A stylish Italian restaurant headed by chef Marco Boscaini. Open-air wood fired pizza oven and home made pastas. Their lasagna is particularly good. Extensive Italian wine list. Open for lunch and dinner. Reservations suggested. 077 300 317. Prego.Samui@amari.com.

Insider tip: There is an air-conditioned dining room towards the back of the restaurant, which is little used. There are usually taxis opposite the Amari hotel, 100 yards away.

Poppies – the restaurant of Poppies Hotel, at the southern end of Chaweng Beach. (Beyond the one-way main road through town.) The restaurant is almost on the beach, serving fine Thai and western food. Thai chef Khun Wantanee Panplum has been with the restaurant since it opened 20 year ago, and the western / international chef Khun Suwit Sunan has been with the restaurant for almost as long. You can sit in the open-sided teak pavilion or outside on the beach terrace. There is also a small beach bar. Reservations suggested. Open for lunch 12 noon – 5pm, and dinner 5pm – 10.30pm. 077 422 419.

Insider tip: There is limited parking in front of the hotel. You follow a winding path through the hotel grounds to get to the restaurant.

Seventy Fahrenheit – Lamai Beach Road, in the center of Lamai town. Owned by French chef Romain Benoist. French-Mediterranean menu plus an extensive Thai menu – the duck yellow curry is recommended. Reasonable prices. Good wine and champagne menu. Open 2pm – 10.30pm. 095 419 9070.

The Page – In the grounds of The Library hotel, on Chaweng Road in town, close to Tropical Murphy's. The Library Hotel is a white minimalist hotel with a red-tiled swimming pool. Walk down a driveway beside the hotel, and you come to "The Page', on a beach terrace. International menu with dishes like tenderloin of Wagyu beef. Also a Thai menu with some unique choices from the royal household, like crispy stewed pork. There is also an eight course set Thai menu. Walk-in wine cellar. Reservations suggested. Open from 7am until 12 midnight, with the kitchen closing at 11pm. There is a separate large modern bar on the main road at the front of the hotel. 077 422 767-8.

Insider tip: The Page is in a busy part of town, with little or no street parking. So take a taxi, or if you drive, there is limited parking on the driveway near the reception office. If you dine on the patio you may need a flashlight or cell phone to read the menu.

The Cliff – between Chaweng and Lamai, on the ring road. Great ocean views. A long-established Samui restaurant which has won Thailand Tatler's 'Best Restaurant' awards for many years. Air conditioned lounge bar and dining on the terrace or in the interior restaurant. Chef Sergio Martelli is well known in Samui, and has been with the restaurant since it opened in 2004. Fresh seafood delivered daily by local fishermen and Australian beef steaks are featured on the menu. The vegetables are organically grown and the herbs are picked from their own herb garden. Entertainment every Friday and Saturday. Open from 12 noon until 10.30pm. Reservations suggested. 077 448 508.

Insider tip: A taxi ride from town. Although there is a great view from the restaurant patio there is no view from the bar. This restaurant is one of the best on Samui but can be pricey.

The Palms Bar & Grill – On Chaweng Road, close to Soi Green Mango, a big lively bar with illuminated palm trees out front. Gastropub meets supper club! Pub favorites like Jack Daniels BBQ ribs, burgers and fajitas. Draft beer, ciders and cocktails. 084 630 4676. ThePalmsSamui.com

Insider tip: Although this restaurant is on the corner of Soi Green Mango it opens much earlier than the late night bars on Green Mango – it is open from around lunch time.

Samui Seafood – on the northern end of Chaweng Beach Road opposite the Samui Spa Resort. Ice cream parlor on one side, thatched bar on the other and a beached boat displaying fresh seafood in the middle. Sit outside on the patio or in the large thatched roof restaurant. There is also a children's playground behind the restaurant. The menu shows photographs of every dish, so that there is no confusion as to what to order! Fresh king prawns or lobster are popular, as is the Samui Seafood Quartet. Thai dancing Monday and Thursday evening. Open for lunch 12 noon – 2pm, and for dinner 6pm until late. 077 429 700.

Noori India – two locations, Chaweng Beach Road opposite the Chaweng Buri Resort, or close to Poppies in south Chaweng. The best Indian restaurants in town, with dishes such as vegetable samosas, Chicken Tika Masala (boneless chicken roasted in the tandoor oven) and Chicken Tawa (chicken cooked in spices and served on a sizzling hot plate). Lots of vegetarian choices also. Thai and Indian beers. Open from 11am until 11.30pm. 077 413 315.

Koh Samui Bars & Clubs

There are well over a hundred bars and clubs in Koh Samui, some catering mainly to Thais, but most with an international clientele. Johnny Walker Black Label Scotch whisky is very popular with Thais. It is said that more Johnny Walker Black is consumed in Thailand than they make in the distillery in Scotland, so go figure! If you are a 'regular' at many popular bars, you can buy a bottle of your favorite drink and leave it at the bar with your name on it. Then next time, ask for it and pay only for ice and mixers. Most places will keep your bottle for up to three months. Some bars employ 'whisky girls' in short dresses, ready to pour Johnny Walker Black Label for their Thai customers.

British readers may be used to ordering beer by the pint or half pint. In Thailand, beer comes in 'large' or 'small' sizes, and the two main domestic makes are Singha and Chang. So you might ask for 'One Singha small', for example.

The center of night life in Koh Samui is Chaweng, with Soi Green Mango and Soi Reggae being the best known areas for bars. Bophut (near the Big Buddha) also has a good selection of bars.

Samui Bars

Legends Bar – A long-established bar in Chaweng Beach, its motto is 'No techno, no Spice Girls, no boy bands!' Live classic rock music seven nights a week.

Bar Ice Samui – behind Soi Green Mango in Chaweng, close to Chaweng Lake. The temperature in this bar is set to below freezing, but they issue warm jackets and fur hats! A great bar for vodka lovers!

Ark Bar – on the beach side of Soi Green Mango, this huge beachfront bar has been serving drinks and music for many years. Open day and night. Fire dancers and fire shows at night.

On Street Bar – Chaweng. A tiny wood and corrugated bar on a small corner lot close to the KC Beach Club Hotel. Recycled furniture (what there is of it!) Inexpensive drinks.

Hard Rock Café – Chaweng. See restaurant listing.

Nikki Beach – Lipa Noi. On the opposite side of the island to Chaweng, but worth the 90 minute trip if you go for the day. A trendy beach club with pools and a DJ.

Good cocktails and restaurant. Live entertainment in the evening. Can be expensive.

Soi Green Mango

Soi Green Mango is in the center of town, and home to the most popular late night bars. If you have heard of Soi Cowboy in Bangkok, or Walking Street in Pattaya, this is the Koh Samui equivalent! Things don't really start here until 8pm – 9pm, and continue until about 2am. There are always taxis available at the end of the street.

The Green Mango Club – Soi Green Mango. The largest and best known bar on the street. It's a large brightly lit warehouse at the end of the soi. Opens late, but then gets very busy.

Dream Girls – Soi Green Mango. The only Thai go-go bar in Soi Green Mango. The girls dance on a small stage, and there are two levels of seating all around. Drinks are about 130 baht and drinks for your 'lady', should you talk to one, are 190 baht. It's a way to tip the dancers.

Inside tip: You can buy ping pong balls for 20 baht each, or a basket for 500 baht, which you throw to the dancers on stage to give them a 'tip' – they exchange the balls for money. Note that you are supposed to throw the ping pong balls *to* the girls, not *at* the girls!

Cubos – Soi Green Mango. A Mexican lounge and bar, with a separate tequila bar. Local DJs play house and hip-hop music. Can get packed late at night.

Galaxy – Soi Green Mango. A go-go bar with 'European' dancers, by which they mean Russian and Eastern European. Much more expensive than other bars in the area, and they also offer bottle service at night club prices.

Inside tip: Service can be offhand if you are not buying a bottle, and the bar can be very quiet unless you go after midnight!

Henry's Africa Bar – Soi Green Mango. The largest and most popular beer bar on the whole street. Pool tables, dance music, beer from 70 baht. Buckets also available. A fun destination if you want a few beers and don't want to be bothered by 'bar girls'.

Our bar – Soi Green Mango. A lively Irish pub with a good selection of drinks – including Guinness!

Viking Bar – Soi Green Mango. This is a popular Swedish, Norwegian and Danish bar, in the Swedish colors of yellow and blue. Inexpensive.

Bars and Clubs

Soi Reggae

Soi Reggae in Chaweng takes its name from the huge and very popular Reggae Pub at the end of the road. There are many bars on the road, some with bar-girl hostesses.

Reggae Pub – Soi Reggae. This is the large well-established nightclub and bar from which the road gets its name. Two stories, with the 'Reggae Restaurant' over the road. Gets busy after 11pm. There is live music some nights.

Coco Bar – Soi Reggae. Israeli owned, with live music and DJs from Israel. Can get packed – mostly people at tables and not dancing. This bar was so successful that the owners opened a second venue in Phuket in 2015.

Samui Pub – Soi Reggae. Lakeside location with a choice of indoor or outdoor seating. There are dancers but this is not a go-go bar, and there is often live music on stage.

Bophut Bars

Bophut is about 30 minutes from Chaweng town, near the Big Buddha. It is an area of small shops, restaurants and bars, open both at lunch time and in the evening. It is popularly known as 'Fisherman's Village'. There are no girly bars or go-go bars or doubtful massage places in Bophut. Finding your way around Fisherman's Village is easy – there is one road in, and when you reach the ocean you can turn right to a few bars and shops, or turn left to the main shopping and bar street.

Coco Tams – Bophut. A popular beach bar in Fisherman's Village, close to the Wharf Samui. Thatched roof buildings, beach and palm trees! Beanbags on the beach and swing seats at the bar. Open day and night.

Gecko Bar – Main Street, Bophut. A Bali-style beachside bar with a resident DJ. They have full moon parties and full moon warm-up parties! Sunday Session Party begins at 2pm.

Insider tip: This bar is part of the Gecko Hotel and has bungalows to rent, but they can get noisy when the parties are in full swing!

Bars and Clubs

The Emerald Irish Bar – Main Street, Bophut. The Emerald is Irish-owned and has photos of old Dublin on the walls. Guinness and Kilkenny are served as well as a good selection of local beers. Good Irish and British food selection.

Inside tip: The kitchen is closed on Mondays. The Billabong Surf Club is a good alternative.

Billabong Surf Club – Main Street, Bophut. Just down the street from the Emerald Irish Bar and with a very similar layout, but this one has an Australian surfing theme. Cheerful staff and excellent menu. View of the ocean from the deck.

Karma Sutra – Main Street, Bophut. A retro bar with Indonesian wooden furniture (with cushions) and Buddha images. Situated at the entrance to Fisherman's Village, by the pier.

Sirocco – Main Street, Bophut. Beatles era music or soft jazz features in this cool bar. Located in a teak former shop-house, close to the pier. Reasonable prices. Closed on Tuesdays.

Live Music Bar

Samui Shamrock – Lamai Beach. Probably the best live music bar in Samui. Good quality rocking Philippino and Thai bands every night of the week. Guinness and Magners cider on draught. Great food, including fish &

chips. Noel and Danny, the Irish owners, will make you very welcome.

Insider tip: The drinks can be a little expensive, but the live music more than makes up for it.

Gay Bars

Koh Samui does have a lively gay scene, though it is much smaller than Bangkok or Pattaya.

The Mix – Chaweng, in the heart of the gay scene near Chaweng Stadium. A small and cozy gay bar with a pool table and good cocktails. Jay the bartender is popular! Several other gay bars in this area.

Pride Bar Samui – Chaweng Beach Road, close to Starz Cabaret. Modern gay lounge, and the staff is very welcoming. Good drinks, cocktails and coffee.

Samui Mojito Lab – Lamai Beach. Gay-friendly lounge bar with a good choice of mojitos as well as wine, cocktails and beer. Drink special 6-8pm.

Ladyboy Shows

Ladyboys are often seen in Thailand. They are young boys who dress up and act like girls, often very realistically. It is said that in Thailand there are three sexes – male, female and ladyboys!

There are several ladyboy cabaret shows in Samui. The 'girls' dress up in exotic costumes, dance and lip sync to music. It's great fun and all are welcome! One of the best known:

Paris Follies Cabaret – Close to Soi Green Mango, down a small soi. A popular and fun Vegas-style ladyboy cabaret show in the center of town. One hour shows at 8pm, 9pm, 10pm and 11pm, though in fact you can go at any time between 8pm and 11pm and see the show. There is a 15 minute intermission between shows. During the intermission the cast assembles outside for photos!

Insider tip: The show cast is great, but the 'waitresses' in tight black dresses have to be seen to be believed!

Karaoke Bars

Insider tip: Some karaoke bars are tourist traps in which you buy drinks for your hostesses and then are presented with a very inflated bar bill when it's time to leave. The charge includes drinks, hand towels and ice, and the expensive privilege of talking to your hostesses!

Shopping in Koh Samui

Shopping in Koh Samui ranges from street markets to a big new shopping mall. Top buys are lacquer, silk, Celadon, tribal artifacts, ceramics and silver jewelry. Bargaining is the norm at market stalls but not in shops or shopping malls.

Samui

Chaweng Walking Street

An evening market in South Chaweng, just off the main street. This is where you can haggle for t-shirts, jeans, sunglasses, copy watches, bags and carved wooden souvenirs. Plan to offer half to two thirds of the price first quoted, and end up paying around two thirds to three quarters of that price. Food court.

Open 4pm – 12 midnight, closed Friday and Sunday.

Insider tip: If you are the first customer of a stall, the stallholder will be eager to make a sale, as that will be 'lucky' for him or her, and they will wave your money across the goods in the stall for good luck. You can get a good deal if you are the first customer of the evening.

Lamai

Lamai Night Plaza is located in the center of Lamai town, the second largest town in Samui. There are stalls selling t-shirts, wooden elephants, sarongs, bags, belts and copy watches. Opens every day from 5pm.

Lamai Walking Street Market is held every Sunday evening on Lamai Beach Road, between the fresh market and the bridge. The road is closed for traffic on this evening, and there are many clothing stalls and food stalls. Sundays from 4.30pm.

Lamai Fresh Market is a local produce market that is open from 5am until 8pm every day. There are fruit and vegetables, grilled fish and meat, curries and deserts! Even if you are not buying fresh produce this can be a fascinating market to see.

Buddy Oriental Plaza is on the Samui ring road next to the Buddy Oriental Samui Beach Resort. There are several restaurants, boutiques and bars, including Mulligans Irish Pub. Open 4.30pm – midnight.

Shopping

Bophut

Bophut and the Fisherman's Village area, 20 minutes from Chaweng, also offers a good selection of small stores, bars and restaurants. There is one road into the village, under the 'Fisherman's Village' arch, and then paid car parking on a dirt lot on the left for motorbikes (20 baht) and cars (40 baht).

On your right is an excellent coffee shop, *Sagatorn Coffee – Barista Academy & Coffee Lab.* At the end of the road, at the beach, turn right for a small group of shops and restaurants or turn left for the main shopping street. There are many tee shirt shops and cafes. Two popular bar restaurants are *Emerald Irish Bar & Restaurant*, and *Billabong Surf Club* (Australian), both with good beach & ocean views. Most shops and restaurants are open 11am – midnight.

Bookstores

There are several new and used bookstores in Samui. Some of the best known:

B2S. Central Festival mall. 077 410-506

Bookazine Chaweng. Chaweng Beach Road. 077 413-908. *Asiabooks.com*

Bookazine Lamai. 124/49 Moo 3. Tambon Maret, Lamai. 077 233-319. *Asiabooks.com*

Drug Stores / Pharmacy

British visitors will be pleased to know that there are four branches of *Boots the Chemist,* the popular British pharmacy, in the Chaweng area. Boots pharmacy stores can now be found in many Thai cities, where most medications are available over the counter without a prescription.

Boots, Central Festival. 2nd floor. 077 410-492. 11am – 11pm.

Boots, Lotus Samui. 077 246-207. 10am – 10.30pm.

Boots, Big C. 077 960-966. 9am – 10.30pm.

Boots, Chaweng Center Plaza. 077 413-724. 11am – 11pm.

Shopping Center & Mall

Central Festival

Central Festival is the largest shopping complex in Samui, with three floors and 90,000 square meters of shopping and dining space – over 200 shops, bars and restaurants. It cannot be missed if you drive through town and is situated between Chaweng Beach Road and Chaweng Lake.

There are four sections of the mall, known as Chaweng Port, Bird Cage, Fisherman Village and Beach Town Market.

Chaweng Port features 21 restaurants and bars, such as Starbucks, Coffee Club, Wine Connection, Copacaba and Swensen's.

Bird Cage is the fashion area of the mall, with about 20 large shops and smaller boutiques, such as Uni-Qlo, Supersports and Jim Thompson.

Fisherman Village is the home to the very large Central Department Store, with many clothing departments and a children's playground with a pirate galleon and seating for parents.

Insider tip: When you pay in a department store, don't expect to immediately get your change in return. They will take your money or credit card and walk to the cash desk with it, which may be some distance away. They will return with the receipt and change several minutes later.

Beach Town Market is situated at the northern end of the complex and has an open-air food court on the ground floor. There are gaming arcades and a movie theater on the second floor.

Opening hours: 11am – 11pm, every day. 077 962-777.

Sports & Fitness in Koh Samui

As the second largest island in Thailand after Phuket it is no surprise that a majority of the sports and fitness activities on Koh Samui are water related.

However, there is an array of other activities available apart from beach and water outings, everything from golf and tennis to ziplining and bungy jumping.

Most activities are easily and quickly arranged, even on short notice unless otherwise noted. For anyone staying at a hotel or resort - as most visitors do - the concierge always is a good place to get prices, locations, make reservations, and any other pertinent information.

Diving, Kayaking and Snorkeling

The south of Thailand has some of the most beautiful beaches and islands in the world, surrounded by crystal clear water and stunning reef and coral formations. As a result, there is hardly a beach on Koh Samui that doesn't have a diving school and/or snorkeling equipment rental shop nestled somewhere.

For anyone who wants to go on a full diving expedition (or just learn how to dive), it probably is best to pick a vendor associated with PADI (Professional Association of Diving Instructors), which guarantees certain professional standards in both instruction and equipment. Others may be and often are just as good, but the PADI affiliation provides a certain comfort level. You know what you're getting.

The nearby Ang Thong Marine National Park includes some 42 nearby islands and a protected area of about 100 square kilometers and makes a great day-trip destination for diving, snorkeling or just sightseeing. Fees depend on the activity and length of time. Only government-approved boats are allowed.

Samui International Diving School, located at the Malibu Resort on Chaweng Beach (Tel: 07741-3050 www.planet-scuba.net) is a good bet for full services. **Easy Divers** also has a location in Chaweng (tel: 07741-3373 www.easydivrs-thailand.com) and offers good deals for beginners. Both outfits, along with many others, offer all kinds of courses and daily dive tours, plus boats meeting international safety standards, equipment and insurance packages. Daily dives, which includes two dives per day in different locations, start at

Sports and Fitness

about 4,000B per person and includes land transportation, breakfast, equipment, lunch and drinks.

Some of the best diving sites in the Ang Thong Marine Park and elsewhere include the Sam Ran Pinnacles, with three submerged pinnacles near Sail Rock, a haven for all sorts of colorful fish. Ko Ra and Koh Losin are two small islands southeast of Koh Samui. Blacktip sharks, manta rays and hard to find loggerhead turtles can be seen here. Ko Tan, also known as No Dog Island, is only 15 kilometers off the southwestern tip of Koh Samui, and a perfect spot for snorkeling. Surrounded by coral and rock reefs, there are 10 beaches on the island. Boats also transport tourists back and forth for a few hundred baht. The island has five restaurants if you want to make a full day of it.

Insider tip: The currents around the San Ran Pinnacles are often strong and this site is recommended only for experienced divers.

Insider tip: Don't be intimidated if you only want to snorkel. There are many more snorkelers than divers in and around Koh Samui. Separate snorkeling trips head out to Ang Thong and elsewhere. With snorkeling, licensing and regulations aren't a concern. If you don't want to be part of a group, some of the better snorkeling off Koh Samui is found along the rocky coast between Chaweng Noiu and Lamai bays. Several shops along Chaweng Beach rent snorkeling gear for about 200B per day.

Blue Stars Kayaking (tel: 07741-3231 www.bluestars.info) takes clients kayaking and snorkeling to the Ang Thong park. The rubber kayaks are great for exploring the caverns hidden beneath the limestone cliffs. The cost is 2,200B for adults and 1,400B for children.

Insider tip: While best time of year for diving is June through August, with fewer squalls to roil the water, diving in this area is excellent all year round.

Cruises

Although a seemingly endless variety of cruises are available, for family fun, try a short cruise on a Chinese junk, **The Fortune** (tel: 07796-0340 www.jonque-fortune.com), which operates out of Fisherman's Village on Boput Beach. It accommodates up to 10 people and also is available for charters. Activities include diving, snorkeling, fishing, island trekking or just enjoying the ride. Day trips range from 2,000 to 3,000B. Sunset cruises are 2,500B.

Sports and Fitness

Golf

As you might expect, golf is limited on Koh Sumui. However, the two courses, designed by renowned golf architect Piraborn Namatra, are beautifully laid out.

Santiburi Samui Country Club – Part of the Santiburi Resort on the north end of the island, it includes a driving range and an 18-hole course that uses the multi-level terrain of the Samui Mountains to create a challenging 6,930-yard 72-par course. With magnificent views of the ocean and beaches, the winding fairways teeter on the edge of cliffs, pass over mountain creeks and cut deep into coconut forests. The fee is 3,000B for hotel guests, 4,000B for non-guests, plus 750B for a mandatory cart and 300B for the caddy, not including the tip. (tel: 0774201700 www.santuburi.com)

Insider tip: You can play nine holes for half the full fee. Duffers Beware: If your typical score runs to 100 or more, you probably will lose several balls on this difficult but beautiful course.

Bophut Hills Golf Club – Opposite the turnoff to Fisherman's Village in the Bophut area of the island, this 9-hole par 3 "pitch and putt" course is a more affordable and relaxed option: the 1,325B fee including greens fees, club rental and caddy. It's 325B less if you bring your own clubs. If you want to go around twice for a full 18 holes, the fee is 2,400B, including clubs and caddy. The setting is beautiful and the course is easier than Santiburi Samui.

Football Golf

Yes, you read that correctly. This family sport at **Samui Football Golf** has become popular on Koh Samui. It needs no clubs, or special skills, and involves kicking a football (a soccer ball, to Americans) down a short course and into a hole. Set at an old coconut plantation just north of Chaweng about five minutes from the Big Buddha, play takes about 90 minutes. 750B for adults and 350B for children. (Tel: 07724-8084 www.samuifootbalgolf.com)

Tennis

Koh Samui is not a tennis hotbed, although it certainly is available if you want it. Most of the major hotels and resorts either have tennis courts on site or can arrange sessions with a hitting partner or match elsewhere. Racquets can be rented and tennis balls rented or purchased.

Sports and Fitness

The primary independent tennis club on the island is the **Koh Samui Tennis Club**, a family owned facility in Bangrak. The two courts have surfaces similar to the courts at the Australian Open. The facility has a small pro shop. It offers Thai and English coaching and provides a hitting partner for 750B per hour. Lessons are 800B per hour. Court time is 250B per hour for two players, 300 B per hour for three players and 350B per hour for four players. (Tel: 8352-91214 www.samuitennis.com)

Insider tip: The club has only two courts, so it is best to make reservations as early as possible.

Ziplining & Bungy Jumping

Ziplining has become globally popular in the last few years and Koh Samui is no exception. If you want to swing through the jungle like Tarzan **Canopy Adventures** is the way to go, with 330 yards of line strung among six tree houses, or platforms. The trip takes at least half the day. Lunch, drinks and fresh fruit are provided. You will be picked up at your hotel, or at some designated spot if you're not staying at a hotel, in a four-by-four vehicle that transports you to the site. The cost is 2,950B, or

2,200B if you register on line. (Tel: 7741-41501 www.canopyadventuresthailand.com).

Samui Bungy is the only operation of its kind on the island. The 50-meter (about 150 feet) drop offers two finishes: One into a pool of water, a refreshing way to end the terror of the fall. The other features the more typical "dry" finish. 1500B. (tel: 07741-4252 www.samuibungy.com) It's in Chaweng on Soi Reggae between the Reggae Pub and EasyKart. Clients are picked up at their hotel.

Massage and Personal Care

Massage and Spas

The art of massage is popular in Koh Samui and certainly less expensive than the United States or Europe – maybe a quarter of the price. Your hotel may be able to arrange for a massage, either in the hotel spa or in your room. There are also many spas available around the island. These are some of the best known:

Samui Ridgeway Luxury Spa. Situated on a mountain, this is a luxury spa with a full range of treatments. Botanical body care and spa products from Simply Samui. 149/1 Moo 3, Tambon Taling Ngam. 081 089-6316.

Samui Dharma Healing Center. A Buddhist educational fasting and spiritual retreat, in business for over 20 years. They offer 7, 10, 14 and 21 day courses. Chinese herbal cleansing and colonic irrigation. Classes in meditation and yoga. Courses begin on a Monday and they suggest that you arrive the day before. Lipa Noi Beach. 077 234-170. *Dharmahealingintl.com*

Insider tip: They say that they are a spiritual retreat and not a spa!

A'Lanna Spa. Situated in Bangrak, in the northeastern part of Samui. Because of their location, they are able to offer spa services for less than other spas. They have their own line of spa products including coconut facial cream, jasmine and tangerine oils. Open 11am – 11pm. 081 797-4100.

Ban Sabai Big Buddha Retreat and Spa. On the beach near to Big Buddha, a compound of Ayutthaya style teak houses and salas. Herbal steam baths, Thai massages, wraps and facials. Indian head massages. Yoga retreats and detox programs. All within sound of the waves. Part of the Ban Sabai Big Buddha Spa Resort. 59 Moo 4, Bophut. 077 245-175. *Bansabairesorts.com.*

Four Seasons Tropical Spa. In central Chaweng, beautifully designed with stone and wooden carvings. Large Jacuzzis and baths. Hot stone massage. Reasonable prices. 11am – 11pm. 077 414-141.

Insider tip: Although the name of this spa is 'Four Seasons' it is not connected with the spa at the Four Seasons resort.

Medical and Personal Services

Dentists

Beauty Smile Dental Clinic. American and Thai-trained dentists work in these four bright dental surgeries. A full range of dental treatments are offered, including implants, crowns, bridges and dental x-rays. Three clinics in Chaweng and one in Lamai Beach. 12/1 Moo 3, Chaweng Beach Road. 077 413-762. *info@beautysmiledetalclinic.com* *Beautysmiledentalclinic.com.*

Skin Care

Rajdhevee Clinic. Aesthetic and dermatologic clinic. Treatments for acne, ant-aging & skin diseases. Laser & beauty treatment. Botox and filler. Skin biopsy. Samui Ring Road, close to Chaweng town center. 077 430-702. *Rcskinclinic.com Samui@rcskinclinic.com.*

Pharmacies

There are four branches of Boots the Chemists in Chaweng, one at Central Festival. (See the shopping chapter.) There is also a Watsons drug store. In Thailand you can get most medications (except opioids) without a prescription.

Hospitals

There are several excellent hospitals in Koh Samui, so there is rarely a need to go to Bangkok for treatment. Most hospital doctors speak English and many of them have attended medical school in the west.

Bangkok Hospital Samui. This is probably the finest hospital in Samui, and nearly all of the doctors speak good English. However, it is also the most expensive hospital in the area. There are well-regarded Bangkok hospitals also in Bangkok, Pattaya and Chiang Mai. 57 Moo 3, Thaweerat Phraldee Rd. 077 429-500. *Samuihospital.com. Info@samuihostpital.com*

Samui International Hospital. One of the island's newest hospitals, SIH offers a wide range of paediatric, gynaecological and cosmetic care, both inpatient and outpatient. Less costly than Bangkok Hospital Samui, and very popular with medical tourist. 90/2 Moo 2, Chaweng Beach Road. 077 230-782. *Sih.co.th info@sih.co.th*.

Medical Tourism

The cost of medical care in Thailand is one quarter to one third the cost of similar care in the USA or Europe. Hospitals are modern and the standard of care is very good. Many people come to Thailand for elective medical care – medical tourism. It is often said that you can pay for the flights, your medical care and a stay in a nice hotel at a total cost that is still far below what you would pay just for medical treatment back home.

Thai Insider: Koh Samui

Thai Food

Everyone knows that Thai food can be hot and spicy, but it's probably more spicy (hotter) in Thailand than you may be used to at home. If you want it less hot, ask for it *mai pet* (not hot).

Despite what you sometimes see on TV, Thais do not eat with chopsticks but use a spoon and fork. Chopsticks are used only for Chinese food and noodle dishes.

Napkins are rarely seen in Thailand. Unless you are in an upscale restaurant there may be a jug on the table with tiny napkins the size of a square of toilet paper. (Or sometimes, an actual roll of toilet paper!)

The dishes in Thailand usually come to the table as they are prepared, not all at once. Most are served family style – the dishes are placed in the middle of the table for everyone to share. Thais often do not order all the dishes at one time, but one at a time, ordering a new dish as they finish the one before.

Place a small heap of rice onto your plate, help yourself to small portions from dishes on the table and place them beside your rice. It's polite to take only a little at a time. Eat with the fork in your left hand to push the food onto your spoon.

If you are a regular in a restaurant you can usually order a bottle of whisky, rum, gin, vodka, etc, and they will keep it with your name on it. Then when you return to the restaurant you can ask for your bottle, and you need only pay for mixers and ice.

Thai cuisine is different in various parts of Thailand. It is often more spicy in the south and northeast, and milder in the midsection, including Koh Samui. Sticky rice (*khao nio*), *som tam* and *khao soy* are also popular in Koh Samui.

Meat is usually chicken (*gai*), pork (*moo*) or beef (*neua*). Also available is seafood (*talay*), shrimp (*goong*) and duck (*ped*). Popular dishes include pork fried with garlic and black pepper, sweet and sour pork and spicy sausage.

Noodles are also popular and come in two types, made from wheat flour (*ba mee*) and made from rice flour (*kuay tiaw*). A popular dish is *paad thai* (pan fried rice noodles with shrimp, peanuts and bean sprouts with a fried egg on top.)

Some Dishes from a Koh Samui Restaurant Menu

- Royal Thai style chicken satay
- Khao soi noodle soup (a local favorite)
- Fermented ground pork fried with elephant garlic
- Stir fried twisted cluster beans with prawns
- Purple flower-shaped dumplings stuffed with chicken
- North-eastern style spicy clear soup with chicken
- Stir fried Thai herbs and chili with herbs
- Grilled marinated pork in hot dish with tamarind sauce
- Stir fried morning glory with oyster sauce and garlic
- Spicy papaya salad
- Steam pork ribs with salted soya beans dip
- Deep fried sun dried pork

The three chilis system

Levels of spiciness in Thai food are indicated by red chilis on the menu. There can be none, one, two or three chilis, depending upon the level of heat. You can request these in Thai if you wish (add krub or kaa to make it more polite):

- No chilis   *Kho mai sai phrik*
- One chili   *Kho sai phrik nit dieo*
- Two chilis   *Kho say prik song met*
- Three chilis   kho say prik saam met

Two or Three Days in Koh Samui

If like many visitors you have only two or three days in Koh Samui on a limited budget, how can you best spend your time? Here is a short list of the 'must do and see' things in Koh Samui.

Around Island Road Trip

This works best if you have a car or motorbike, and can easily be done in a day. Get an island map, available when you land at the airport, or at a hotel or bookstore.

Begin in Chaweng, if your hotel is nearby, and take the 4171 road leading north out of the town. It loops around and soon reaches Wat Phra Yai, the Big Buddha, a twelve meters high seated Buddha that can be seen from far away. There are steep steps leading up to the Buddha, but the view from ground level is good.

Spend an hour walking up to the Big Buddha and the shops nearby. Then turn left out of Big Buddha and left again after half a mile to Wat Plai Laem. (You are back tracking a little, but this is the easiest way to find it.) Wat Plai Lem features a striking 18 arm image of Guavin, the goddess of mercy and compassion, and also this statue!

Go back onto the 4171 road, turn left and go to Bophut, the Fisherman's Village. You can park on the left as you enter the village (small fee), which has many shops and restaurants making it a good place to stop for lunch.

Return to the main road, and turn right onto the 4169 road, the main island ring road taking you through Mae Nam and Bang Por, past the Four Seasons Hotel on the right (a good place for a drink if your budget will stretch to that!) Then to the town of Nathon, where ferries from the mainland stop.

Insider tip: Nathon has a system of one-way streets, but if you are going south through the town (as on this trip), you keep to the main road and are not affected. If you go north through Nathon you are diverted onto the one-way streets.

Turn right onto the 4174 road if you want to go to the Nikki Beach Club, a well-known beach club with pools and a DJ If not continue on the 4169 road until you come to Wat Khunaram, where there is the famous mummified monk in a glass case.

Monk Luang Pho Poo Rerm died at the age of 87 in 1976 while meditating and ever since his body has been displayed in an upright glass case in the temple.

Continue on the 4169 road and you come to the well-known landmarks of Hin Ta and Hin Yai, the 'Grandfather and Grandmother rocks', with rocks shaped like male and female genitalia. (See the 'Things to do' chapter.)

The town of Lamai is next, with many hotels and restaurants. Continue on the 4169 road and turn right onto the 4171 road which takes you back through the center of Chaweng to your starting point.

Safari Boat to Koh Phangan

This is an all-day trip to a small neighboring island. You are picked up from your hotel at 7.30am, have a light breakfast at the safari boat office, and then take a speed boat for the 20 minute ride to Koh Phangan island.

Once there, you visit the Than Sadet Waterfall, the Thai Meditation Temple, and elephants, including a chance to feed and play with the baby elephants!

Lunch is served at a popular restaurant, then you see a Thai Heritage Show with food tasting, and learn about local life and culture. There is also an archery range.

Finally, speedboat and minivan transfer back to your hotel.

077 447-700. Safariboat.info. info@safariboat.info.

Island Safari City Tour

This package minibus tour covers much of the same ground as the around island tour that you can yourself. But you don't have to drive!

Tour includes: Elephant trekking, elephant show, fish spa, Big Buddha Temple, Plai Laem Temple, Grandfather & Grandmother rocks, mummified monk, Namuang

Waterfall, Nathorn Town. Adult 800 baht, child 600m baht. Airconditioned minibus. Island Safari. 077 425-563 *IslandSafariTour.com*

Samui Adventure

A half day tour which includes: Elephant trekking, Namuang Falls (swimming), monkey show, Sila Ngu Pagoda, mummified monk, Grandfather & Grandmother rocks, tasty Thai food. Pick up from your hotel at about 11am, return about 5pm. Adult 1,750 baht. Child 1,400 baht. 077 424-729. *Samuijungletrip.com*. The same company also runs ATV adventure tours and paint ball contests.

ECO Tour

This is a more extensive eight hour tour, beginning with pickup from your hotel at 8.15am.

Tour includes: Plai Leam Temple, Grandfather & Grandmother rocks, coconut house plantation, rubber plantation – tapping a rubber tree. Elephant trekking, with free photo.

A Thai buffet lunch is followed by a visit to an elephant village, Namuang Waterfall II, the highest waterfall in Samui, 80 meters high. Then baby elephants bathing & baby elephants show. Monkeys at work. Kayaking through a mangrove forest, and finally return to your hotel.

Adults 1,950 baht, children 1,600 baht. 077 424-098. *Namuangsafarisamui.com.* Email: *Namuangsafarisamui@gmail.com.*

Thai Insider: Koh Samui

Staying Longer in Koh Samui

Koh Samui is great for a short visit, but what about staying longer? Perhaps a month or several months? The Thai 'no visa required' tourist entry gives you permission to stay in Thailand for up to thirty days (29 nights). To stay longer you need to apply to your local Thai embassy or consulate for a visa. Twelve month visas are available, though they usually have a requirement to check in with the local Thai immigration office (or leave the country and re-enter) every 90 days.

Or if you have a thirty day stay you can make a 'visa run' to a neighboring border before your time is up, and re-enter Thailand for another 30 days. Malaysia is the closest country to Koh Samui, and Singapore is also very easy to reach.

Koh Samui is easily accessible from within Thailand and overseas. There are direct flights from Bangkok, Chiang Mai, Phuket and Pattaya within Thailand, and overseas from Singapore, Hong Kong and Kuala Lumpur.

You can rent an apartment or house for a month at a time, starting at about 30,000 baht. (About $1,000).

You can also buy an apartment or house if you wish to stay longer. These properties can be easily rented when you are not there.

Insider tip: The best-known agent for rental and sales of villas and apartments in Samui is IVL Property. 077 417-113 *ivlproperty.com*.

Some more apartment and villa rental agents:

Century 21 Zazen	089 866-8931
Horizon Homes	077 417-005
Klik Asia	089 866-4515
Koh Phangan Lux Villas	077 374-354
Koh Samui Properties	077 484-770
Luxury Villas Samui	084 842-7506
Luxury Villas Siam	087 922-8381
Remax Island Real Est	080 041-0420
Sage Land & House	089 016-9750
Samui Escapes	077 425-136
Villa Mya	077 417-113

Staying Longer

Insider tip: If you rent your house or apartment, professional photographs make the process much easier. The top property photographer on Samui for the past 15 years is Claudio Images. 08 7270-4972 *Fantasyatwork@yahoo.com.*

Development on the island has been mostly on the northern and eastern coasts, where the major towns and the airport are situated. However, in recent years the west coast has seen more new hotels, and now housing developments too.

Buying a house or land

Land and house properties in Thailand are measured in Rai, Ngan and Wah.

 1 Wah is 4 square meters or 43 square feet.

1 Ngan is 100 Wah or 400 square meters or 4,300 square feet.

4 Ngan is 1 Rai or 1600 square meters or 17,000 square feet.

2.5 Rai is 1 Acre. (Not used in Thailand but given here for comparison).

Usually, title deeds are given as a Chanote. This title has legal documents of rights of ownership and can be sub divided into smaller lots. There are other types of deeds, but the Chanote is the most popular and easiest to understand.

Apartment prices usually start at about 3 million Thai Baht (about $100,000) and go up from there. 50% financing is often available.

The popularity of real estate in Samui has given rise to many supporting professional services, such as English speaking lawyers, realtors and builders.

Schools

There is a wide choice of well-established nurseries and schools in Samui. These include the International School Samui (ISS), the British International School and Lamai International School. These schools mostly follow the British educational system. There are also many sporting clubs around the island, and the Coco Splash or Pink Elephant amusement park.

Westerners often move to Thailand to teach English and choose Koh Samui because it is quieter and more beautiful than Bangkok. An average teaching salary in Koh Samui at a government school is usually about 20,000 baht a month ($650).

Useful Koh Samui Information

Electricity

Thailand uses 220 volts, 50 cycles, and uses sockets that accept two pin flat or round plugs. Therefore phone chargers with US plugs will work, and those from the UK require an adapter. Appliances such as heated hair tongs and hair dryers designed for US voltage will not work, as the Thailand voltage is higher.

Phone numbers

Koh Samui phone numbers (land lines) begin with the 077 area code, and then six digits, for example 077 555-123. This looks like 'one number is missing' to western eyes, but it is correct. Mobile phone numbers have an area code like 069 or 086, and then seven digits, for example 069 555-1234. Bangkok numbers begin with 02.

The international dialing code is 001. Therefore for international calls you would dial the following:

USA   001 1

UK	001 44
Canada	001 1
Australia	001 61
New Zealand	001 64
Ireland	001 353

To call Thailand from abroad you would dial +66 then the regional area code without the leading zero, then the number. For example, to dial the Koh Samui number 077-555-123 you would dial +66 77-555-123.

Sim Cards

To make local calls more cheaply, replace the SIM card in your phone with a Thai SIM card, and get a Thai number. However, if you do this, of course your 'home' mobile number will no longer be active. You can buy a prepaid SIM card from an AIS, True or DTAC store, and you can add money to your card at any 7-11 store in town.

Some Useful Koh Samui Phone Numbers

| Information | 1133 |
| Immigration office | 077-421-069 |

Useful Information

Samui Airport	077-425-012
Tourism Authority	077-420-504
Samui Hospital	077-421-230
International Hospital	077-422-272
Bandon Hospital	077-245-236
Ambulance	077-421-444
Fire Dept	199
Police	191
Tourist Police	077-421-281
Tourist Police Emgcy	1699
Bangkok Bank	077-421-105
Thai Military Bank	077-420-360
Siam Commercial Bank	077-420-186
Thai Farmers Bank	077-421-200
Thai International	02-513-0121
Silk Air	02-236-0440

Embassies & Consulates

Most government offices in Thailand operate 8.30am to 4.30pm Monday to Friday. Foreign embassies and consulates may have different opening hours.

Bangkok embassies

US embassy. 95 Wireless Rd, Bangkok. 02 205-4000

UK embassy. 14 Wireless Rd, Bangkok. 02 305-8333

Canadian embassy. 15/F Abdulrahim Place, Bangkok. 02 636-0560

Australian embassy. 37 Th Sathorn Tai, Bangkok. 02 344-6300

New Zealand embassy. 87 Wireless Rd, Bangkok. 02 254-2530

Singapore embassy. 129 Th Sathorn Tai, Bangkok. 02 286-2111

Airports

The code for the main Bangkok airport (Suvarnabhumi) is BKK, and for Koh Samui it is USM. Note that the 'old' Bangkok airport, Don Muang (also known as Don Mueang), is still operating, and the code for that is DMK. Don Muang is the regional hub for Nok Air, Thai Air Asia, Thai Lion Air and Orient Thai Airways. Suvarnabhumi (the main international airport) is the regional hub for Thai airways, Bangkok Airways and almost all of the other airlines operating in Thailand.

Insider tip: Flights from Bangkok to Koh Samui usually depart from Suvarnabhumi airport. Koh Samui has direct international flights, so it is not always necessary to arrive or depart Thailand via Bangkok. Koh Samui's direct flights include Hong Kong and Singapore.

Changing Money

You can change money from your local currency to Thai baht at your hotel, or at one of the many 'Exchange' windows in town. They will not accept torn, crumpled or defaced notes, so bring clean new notes if you can. Thai baht notes come in values of 20, 50, 100, 500 and 1,000 baht

Credit cards

Credit cards are widely accepted at larger stores and hotels in Thailand, particularly Visa and Mastercard, and to a lesser extent, American Express. Cash only is accepted in small stores and all markets. Small bills are useful. Credit cards can be used in most ATMs to withdraw Thai currency (which will usually be in 1,000 baht notes). Should you lose your card, call one of these numbers:

Visa: 001 800-441-3485

Mastercard: 001 800-11-887-0663.

American Express: 02 273-5222

Diner's Club: 02 238-3660

Some Thai Phrases

Thai is a tonal language – words change depending on how you say them, for example with a rising or falling tone. So written Thai words and phrases are just a starting point. You need to hear how Thais actually say those words to be better understood.

The most important Thai phrases to learn are those for 'Hello' and 'Thank you', with Thai numbers probably being the next easiest to learn.

To make a Thai phrase more polite, you end it with 'krub' (sometimes sounds like 'krap') if you are a man, and 'kaa' if you are a woman. Note that it is not whether you are speaking to a man or a woman that is important here, it is whether *you* are a man or a woman.

Hello and thank you

Hello   Sawasdee krub (male), Sawasdee kaa (female)

Thank you   kob koon (krub/kaa)

Numbers

Thai Insider: Koh Samui

Zero	Soon
One	Nung
Two	Song
Three	Sam
Four	Si
Five	Haa
Six	Hok
Seven	Jet
Eight	Bat
Nine	Kow
10	Sip
20	Yee sip (not song sip)
30, 40, 50 etc	Sam sip, Si sip, Haa sip, etc
100	Nung roi
200, 300 etc	Song roi, Si roi, etc
1000	Nung phan

Some Thai Phrases

Insider tip: The Thai word for 5 is haa, so when texting each other they often end the text with '555' – 'Ha ha ha!'

Days of the Week

Day	Wan
Monday	Wan Jaan
Tuesday	Wan Ang Karn
Wednesday	Wan Put
Thursday	Wan Paluehas
Friday	Wan Sook
Saturday	Wan Sao
Sunday	Wan Ar-tit

Dining

Table	Tao
Chair	Gao Eie
Plate	Jarn
Spoon	Shon

Fork	Sorm
Knife	Meed
Bowl	Charm
Glass	Gaew
Napkin	Pa Ched Pak
Plain water	Nam plao
Ice	Nam khoeng
Orange juice	Nam som khan

Colors

Color	See
Red	See Daeng
Yellow	See Leung
Pink	See Chom Poo
Green	See Kiew
Orange	See Som
Blue	See Fah
White	See Kao

Some Thai Phrases

Black	See Dum
Purple	See Muang

Useful Phrases

How are you?	Sabai dee reu?
Never mind	Mai pen rai
I cannot speak Thai	Phood Thai mai dai
Please speak slowly	Phood cha-cha
I don't understand	Mai kao jai
Where is the restroom?	Hong nam yoo tee nai?
Very expensive	Paeng maag
The bill please	Gep taang (krub/kaa)
Thank you very much	Kob khun maak
Today	Wan ni
Tomorrow	Prung ni
Yesterday	Mua wan ni

Places

Airport	Sanam bin
Railway station	Sa-tanee rot fai
Police station	Sa-tanee tum-ruad
Hotel	Rong-raem
Hospital	Rong-payabaan
Market	Talaad

Authors' Bios

Granville Kirkup is a former business and popular restaurant owner. He has been visiting Koh Samui for almost thirty years, and has seen it change much over the years. Ten years ago he purchased a condominium in Chiang Mai and he now lives there for part of every year. Married with two children, he lives with his wife, Sidney, in California when they are not in Thailand. *Granvillekirkup2017@gmail.com*

Thai Insider: Koh Samui

Robert Wisehart is the author of eight novels, including the "Cabo" private detective series, and three historical novels based on the life of Sam Houston. A former award-winning print, radio and television journalist, his is a frequent Thailand visitor and lives with his wife, Dana, in Santa Fe, New Mexico. *Robertwisehart.com*

Acknowledgments

Many locals, expats and frequent Thailand visitors have helped to provide the information and Insider Tips in this book. Among these are David Rueda, Julie Hastings, Armelle Chungchareonsuk-Pennors, Sidney Kirkup, Dana Wisehart, Louise Kirkup, John Rees, Arthur Wickson, Tricia Freeman, Pamela Terrones, Aimee Richter, Katie Rollins, Jeff Rollins, Susan Davis, David Schmidt, Gerald Maguire MD, Connie Yeaman, Alam Horner, Jessica Scott, Bill Horner, Barbara Haywood, Pakin Ployphicha, Toby Allen, Patcharin Toon, Denise Gray, Richard Kirkup, Monica Hampton, Philip Smith, Sophie & Larry Cripe, Don Yeaman, Richard Dixon, Manat Chowmuang, Harriett Stanley, Cheryl Hoenemeyer, Annie Frome, Howard & Annie Freedland.

Comments, updates and corrections are much appreciated, and will be acknowledged here in a future edition. Please send an email to the authors at *GranvilleKirkup2017@gmail.com*.

Thai Insider: Koh Samui

Further Reading

Thai Insider: Chiang Mai. An Insider's Guide to the Best of Thailand. Granville Kirkup & Robert Wisehart. Rimping Publishing Company. *Amazon.com* GranvilleKirkup2017@gmail.com.

Chiang Mai: The Top 10. The best things to do on a visit to Chiang Mai, Thailand. Granville Kirkup & Robert Wisehart. Rimping Publishing Company. *Amazon.com* GranvilleKirkup2017@gmail.com.

Chiang Mai Stories: Adventures in Thailand. Granville Kirkup. Rimping Publishing Company. *Amazon.com* GranvilleKirkup2017@gmail.com.

Retiring in Thailand. Live in paradise for pennies on the dollar. Sunisa Wongdee Terlecky & Philip Bryce. Paiboon Bangkok Publishing. paiboonpublishing@gmail.com *Paiboonpublishing.com*

Burma's Golden Triangle. Andre & Louis Boucard. Asia Books. 5 Sukhumvit Soi 61, Bangkok. PO Box 40. Bangkok 10110.

Thailand Customs & Culture. Roger Jones. (One of a series on customs and culture in different countries). Kuperand. *Culturesmart.co.uk*

Successful Living in Thailand. Roger Welty. Asia Books. Information@asiabooks.com *Asiabooks.com*

What's What in a Wat. Carol Stratton. Silkworm Books. Chiang Mai. info@silkwormbooks.com. *Silkwormbooks.com*

Ancient Luang Prabang. Denise Haywood. River Books. Bangkok. riverps@ksc.th.com *Riverbooksbk.com*

Lightning Source UK Ltd.
Milton Keynes UK
UKHW02f2058260418
321722UK00035B/826/P